Life of the Butterfly

Life of the Butterfly

by Heiderose and Andreas Fischer-Nagel

A Carolrhoda Nature Watch Book

 Carolrhoda Books, Inc./Minneapolis

Thanks to Mr. Jerry Heaps, Registered Professional Entomologist, for his assistance with this book

This edition first published 1987 by Carolrhoda Books, Inc.
Original edition published 1983 by Kinderbuchverlag KBV Luzern AG,
Lucerne, Switzerland, under the title BUNTE WELT DER
SCHMETTERLINGE: DAS TAGPFAUENAUGE
Copyright © 1983 Kinderbuchverlag KBV Luzern AG
Translation from the German © 1983 by J.M. Dent & Sons Ltd.
Adapted by Carolrhoda Books, Inc.

Manufactured in the United States of America

This book is available in two editions:
Library binding by Carolrhoda Books, Inc.
Soft cover by First Avenue Editions
241 First Avenue North
Minneapolis, Minnesota 55401

LIBRARY OF CONGRESS CATALOGING-IN-PUBLICATION DATA

Fischer-Nagel, Heiderose.
   Life of the butterfly.

   Translation of: Bunte Welt der Schmetterlinge.
   "A Carolrhoda nature watch book."
   Includes index.
   Summary: Introduces the physical characteristics,
habits, and behavior of butterflies and some of the
different species.
   1. Butterflies—Juvenile literature. [1. Butterflies]
I. Fischer-Nagel, Andreas. II. Title.
QL544.2.F5613   1987   595.78'9   86-23217
ISBN 0-87614-244-7 (lib. bdg.)
ISBN 0-87614-484-9 (pbk.)

   4   5   6   7   8   9   10   97   96   95   94   93   92   91   90   89

Butterflies are one of the most delightful signs of summer. They flit through fields and gardens, alighting on one flower briefly before going on to the next. Even before butterflies appear, though, caterpillars are out— eating steadily as they crawl from leaf to leaf. A long time ago, caterpillars and butterflies were thought to be two entirely unrelated creatures. Many legends surrounded the beautiful butterfly. One such legend led people to believe that witches took the form of butterflies so that they could fly into homes to steal butter and milk. This is a probable source for the butterfly's name. Another common belief was that butterflies were the souls of people, released upon death.

Now we know that caterpillars and butterflies are the same insect at different stages of development. It is hard to believe that a fleshy caterpillar can develop into something as graceful as a butterfly. The process of **metamorphosis**, or transformation, is similar for most other insects, but none emerge from their periods of rest so dramatically changed as the butterfly.

Many different **species**, or kinds, of butterfly exist throughout the world. One species of butterfly, the peacock butterfly, is a common sight in the fields and towns of Europe and Asia. It can be recognized by its rust-red coloring and the four multi-colored eyespots on the wings. These eyespots resemble the markings on a peacock's tail feathers, giving this butterfly its name.

Peacock butterflies belong to a **family**, or group, of butterflies along with many other species—some of which live in North America. The butterflies in the same family with the peacock butterfly have the scientific name *Nymphalidae*, although they are commonly called brush-footed butterflies. The way to identify a brush-footed butterfly is by looking for its **brush feet**, or extremely short front legs. All butterflies have three pairs of legs, but brush-footed butterflies have only two pairs that operate as walking legs. The third pair, or brush feet, are useless for walking or for grasping a surface. They are covered with sensory hairs that are taste organs used to help locate food.

Some of the members of this butterfly family that live in North America as well as in Europe are the tortoiseshell, the red admiral, and the painted lady. In this book we will look closely at the life cycle of the peacock butterfly, which is similar to that of other brush-footed butterflies.

There are, of course, male and female butterflies. The scales on their wings help butterflies find mating partners by both smell and sight. The scales are connected to **glands** that emit substances with an odor. Male and female butterflies are attracted to each other by the different smells that these glands give off. Butterflies can also see the colorful patterns made by the wing scales, which helps them to find mates of their own species. Pairing takes place in early summer, soon after the butterflies emerge from **hibernation**, or long winter rest.

During mating, the male deposits his **sperm**, or male reproductive cells, into the female. Small **claspers**, which are clawlike structures at the end of the male's abdomen, are used to join the male and female while they are mating. Male and female spend from thirty minutes to several hours with their hindquarters attached until all the sperm have been transferred to the female.

Within a few hours after mating, the female begins to lay her eggs. The female peacock butterfly lays her eggs on a plant that will provide the right food for the caterpillars that will hatch. She can find the right food by "tasting" the leaves through the sense organs on her brush feet.

Stinging nettle leaves are the favorite food of the peacock butterfly caterpillar and of several other brush-footed butterflies. On the underside of the nettle leaves, the female lays a small pile of about 250 eggs. As she lays the eggs, she **fertilizes** them with the sperm that she has stored in her body since mating. Each egg has a tiny hole through which the sperm enters. The eggs look like miniature gooseberries, each one being smaller than the head of a pin.

This egg-laying female has folded her wings together and looks so plain that you might have thought she was an entirely different type of butterfly. Many brush-footed butterflies have scallop-edged wings that are brightly colored on top with dull undersides.

A female peacock butterfly will deposit several bunches of about 250 eggs throughout the remaining two weeks of her life until she has laid a total of about 1,500 eggs. A sticky substance that is produced by the female's body is used to attach the eggs to the leaf. This fluid hardens, gluing the eggs firmly in position and protecting them from the cold and from drying out.

The eggs in this photograph are about seven days old. You can see the black heads of the **larvae** through the egg shells.

14

This photograph shows the stage of development that has been reached after about eight days.

The larvae, or caterpillars, chew their way out of the eggs and crawl onto the nettle leaf. The caterpillars start eating right away, beginning with their egg shells.

The caterpillar's body is made up of 13 equal-sized sections known as **segments**. One segment includes the head.

While still small, the caterpillars keep close together as a protection against **predators** such as birds and other insects. One caterpillar is an easy target for predators, but a group looks like a large, inedible creature. As they grow larger, they will begin to spread out, clustering together again at night to keep warm.

The caterpillars eat and eat until all that remains of a leaf is a skeleton. They then spin a very fine web which hangs like a silken net from the remains of the leaf. As they crawl over this flimsy platform, they leave their waste droppings everywhere.

17

Since the caterpillar is constantly eating, it soon grows too big for its skin. The skin bursts, starting to split behind the head and opening down the body to allow the caterpillar to crawl out. This process of shedding the skin is known as **molting**. Molting times vary from species to species.

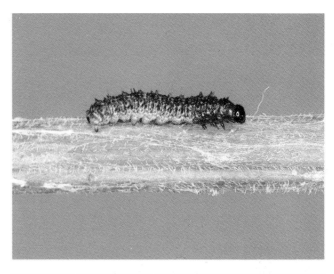

The molt begins for peacock caterpillars when the caterpillars are about six days old. By this time, they have become a little darker in color.

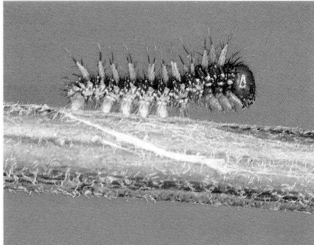

This caterpillar has just shed its old skin. Its body is covered with bristly hairs that serve as sensory organs to help the caterpillar feel its way about.

After a few minutes, these hairs change color, and the caterpillar becomes dark, except for a few white dots. As soon as its new skin has dried, the caterpillar starts eating again with fresh energy.

The caterpillars of the peacock butterfly are "social caterpillars" that crowd together for any period of time that interrupts their constant eating. They come together to molt, remaining crowded together for only a short time while their new skin dries. Once again, this clustering serves to protect them from predators.

This photograph shows a caterpillar up close, making it appear much larger than it actually is. Its head is on the left. Each of the first three body segments behind the head bears a pair of black legs tipped with claws. These claws help the caterpillar hold on tightly to the leaf while feeding. Further back are five pairs of **prolegs**, or fleshy walking legs, that are pale orange in color. The tips of the prolegs have a circle of curved hooks that act as tiny suction pads. They enable the caterpillar to cling to smooth surfaces.

A large magnifying glass makes it possible to examine a caterpillar closely. Since a caterpillar's main task is eating, its mouth must work well. Its powerful jaws, with razor-sharp cutting edges, gnaw away an entire leaf, piece by piece.

There is not always enough food for every caterpillar. The caterpillar of the peacock butterfly eats only weeds. Unfortunately people usually try to destroy all garden weeds, leaving less food for the hungry caterpillars. Many caterpillars of the peacock butterfly are also killed by poisonous sprays used against insects that harm fruit trees or vegetable plants. Peacock butterflies, therefore, are likely to be found in large numbers only in areas where weeds grow and no poisons are used.

As is true with most insects, there is a good chance that many butterfly offspring will be the victims of scarce food supply, poison, predators, or bad weather. For this reason, butterflies and other insects need to lay large numbers of eggs to increase the chances of at least some offspring surviving.

Even with a magnifying glass, the caterpillar's five or six small pairs of eyes are hardly visible. These small **ocelli**, or simple eyes, on either side of the head can barely distinguish dark from light. The caterpillar's eyes do not need to be highly developed since the caterpillar uses its senses of touch and taste to find the right food.

Here, once again, we can see the skin splitting open from the head downward. Pumping movements help the caterpillar slip out of its old skin. It does not move until its new, damp skin has had time to dry.

The caterpillar phase of the peacock butterfly lasts only five weeks. The caterpillar will molt a total of three times before this stage ends. Other caterpillars molt as few as two and as many as ten times before entering the next stage of their life cycle.

During the next stage of the butter-fly's life cycle, the caterpillar becomes a **pupa**, entering into an inactive stage while it undergoes internal changes. The pupal stage lasts 10 to 14 days.

The caterpillar finds a sheltered place, usually on a twig, and deposits a sticky liquid from its body to form a sort of silk pad. The caterpillar then hangs motionless upside down from its point of attachment (1).

Its skin appears to shrink. Then it begins to split apart on the head as if molting. Indeed, sometimes this is called the last molt (2). The skin continues to split, taking about two minutes to split down to the hind end (3).

Now the pupa begins to appear. It wriggles and writhes until the skin falls off. At first, the pupa, a greenish yellow color, is still soft (4). Immediately, a hard, protective shell, called a **chrysalis**, or pupal covering, begins to form over the soft pupa. The chrysalis is a darker color of green (5). The development of the butterfly is completed within the chrysalis (6).

⑦ ⑧ ⑨

Even before it breaks out of the chrysalis, the developing butterfly's wing markings can be seen through the sides of the case. At this stage the chrysalis is bluish in color (7).

After 10 to 14 days, the chrysalis suddenly bursts open as though it has been unzipped (8).

The peacock butterfly emerges head first, in a matter of seconds, from the chrysalis (9).

The butterfly uses a lot of energy in working its way out of the chrysalis (10). At first its wings remain pressed together as the newly emerged butterfly grips the empty chrysalis. Little by little a bloodlike fluid is pumped from the tiny body into hollow wing **veins**, or tubes, until the wings are fully expanded. The butterfly then spreads its wings out to dry and harden. The fluid is withdrawn from the wing veins, and the butterfly is ready to fly (11 and 12).

A butterfly can take any-where from two minutes to several hours to unfold its wings, depending upon the species. Usually the butterfly is ready to fly about a half hour after emerging from the chrysalis.

Most butterflies rest with their wings closed. By folding its wings and displaying their drab undersides, as shown here, the peacock butterfly helps protect itself against predators. In this way, it is less noticeable during this vulnerable time.

This is a close-up view of the butterfly's head. Unlike the simple eyes of the caterpillar, the butterfly's **compound eyes**, which are made up of many small lenses, are easily seen in a close-up look. These compound eyes do more than distinguish light and dark; they are able to give the butterfly a rough color picture of its surroundings.

The **proboscis**, or feeding tube, is rolled up. When the butterfly extends the long proboscis, it can reach deep into flowers to suck out the sweet **nectar**. The brush feet, covered with sensory hairs, are clearly visible in this photograph, jutting up on either side of the rolled-up proboscis, as the white arrow shows.

The **antennae** bear sense organs that the butterfly uses to smell. Using their eyes, antennae, and the sensory hairs on their legs and bodies, butterflies have no trouble finding their way around.

Early in the morning, when flowers are wet with dew, butterflies are still. A butterfly cannot fly if its body temperature is less than 86 degrees F (30 degrees C). If the outside temperature is colder than this, it must sit in the sun, or flutter its wings to warm up.

As soon as it has been warmed by the sun's rays, a butterfly spreads its wings and flies here and there from flower to flower. The reason for such a flight pattern is that a butterfly can see the colors and patterns on flowers. It recognizes certain flowers, and concentrates on those flowers that are full of nectar that can be reached by the butterfly's proboscis.

The length of the proboscis can be seen only when it is fully extended as the butterfly sucks the nectar from a flower. To help you see it, some petals were taken off the flower in the photograph to the right.

Butterflies play an important part in the **pollination** of flower blossoms. When a butterfly lands on a flower in order to drink the nectar, the yellow **pollen**, containing male reproductive cells, sticks to the hairs covering the butterfly's body. When the butterfly flies to another flower of the same kind, it brings the pollen to another blossom, where the pollen sticks to the female parts of that flower. The uniting of the female and the male reproductive cells is called fertilization. Plants with flowers cannot produce the seeds or fruit necessary for new plant growth without fertilization.

The butterfly's wings are clear **membranes** covered with colorful scales. Some of the scales contain **pigments**, or color-creating chemicals. Scales that are black, brown, red, white, and yellow get their color from pigment.

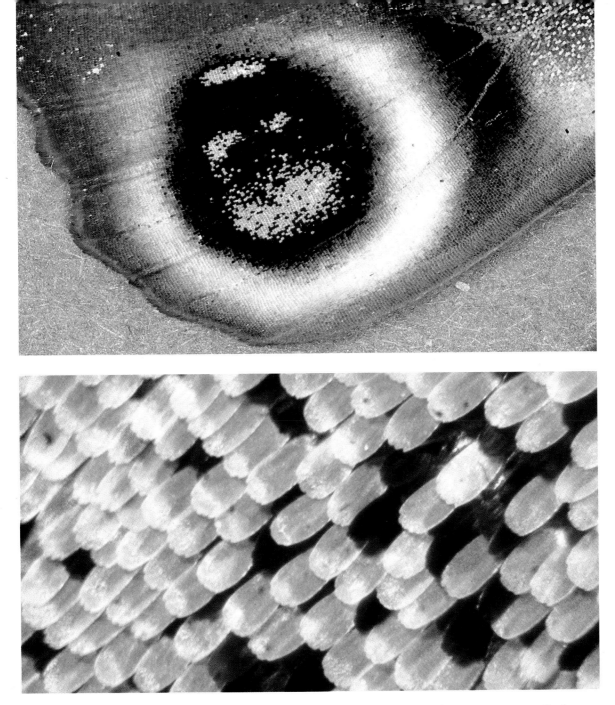

The other colors of shimmering blue and pink are created from light reflecting from the surface of the scales. All of the scales overlap to form the colorful, glittering pattern characteristic of the peacock butterfly.

The underside of brush-footed butterflies' wings show none of the brilliant colors that appear on the top of the wings. When folded, the wings have a dry, leaflike or barklike appearance that helps them to blend in with their surroundings so that they can escape the notice of predators. This protection is useful for this family of butterflies because most brush-footed butterflies hibernate as adults. During hibernation they would be very vulnerable to attack without this **camouflage**, or protective coloring.

The coloring of the peacock butterflies' wings has a second way of working to protect the butterflies. If a bird approaches a butterfly that is showing the dull undersides of its wings, the butterfly may open its wings suddenly and display the bright colors and eyespots on the top of its wings. This may startle the bird so that it flies away.

As summer draws to an end, butterflies become more and more sluggish. There are noticeably fewer of them about, and those that remain have wings that are torn and frayed, showing the effects of the wind, rain, and general wear.

Most peacock butterflies live for only two weeks to one month, and each year only a small number survive to hibernate through the winter. They find a protected spot where they will blend in, such as the dark corners of a porch or room, and wait out the winter. When spring comes they will find a mate and start the cycle all over again.

There are about 20,000 species of butterfly in the world. The 3 orange, white, and black butterflies pictured here are all brush-footed butterflies. You can see their small brush feet sticking out from their heads, between their antennae.

The butterfly in the top photograph on the opposite page is a tortoiseshell butterfly, so called because the pattern on its wings vaguely resembles the design on some tortoises' shells. The white spots along the bottom edge of the wing can appear blue when they reflect light in a certain way. The tortoiseshell pictured here is called a small tortoiseshell butterfly and is commonly found in Europe and Asia. There are two species of tortoiseshell butterfly found in the United States, the American tortoiseshell and the California tortoiseshell. They have markings similar to the small tortoiseshell.

Like the peacock butterfly, the red admiral butterfly, pictured on the bottom left of the opposite page, is fond of nettle plants. These brush-footed butterflies are found in North America, Europe, northern Africa, and Asia. They are **migratory** butterflies, flying north in the spring or summer to lay their eggs. The butterflies that eventually come from those eggs fly south in the fall in search of a warmer winter climate.

Another nettle-loving butterfly is the painted lady butterfly, pictured above. This species is found all around the world in countries with moderate climates, except in South America. Like the red admiral butterfly, painted lady butterflies are migratory, with the same seasonal pattern of migration as the red admiral.

Monarch butterflies, pictured on the opposite page, live on many continents, but the greatest concentrations of monarchs are found in North America. They are best known for their spectacular migrations. Huge flocks of monarchs, sometimes millions of butterflies, fly from southern Canada or northern United States to California, Florida, Mexico, and other warm places for the winter. Each year the monarchs gather together to winter in the same locations they wintered during the previous year. With the coming of spring, they return to their northern homes.

Monarch caterpillars eat milkweed plants, which have a milky juice in their stems that is poisonous to many creatures. When the caterpillar becomes a butterfly, this poison is still in its body, so when a bird eats a monarch, the bird will become sick. This protects the monarch butterfly because the bird will then avoid all butterflies with the monarch's coloring. The viceroy, a nonpoisonous butterfly that looks like the monarch, is also avoided by birds.

Some of the more brilliantly colored butterflies are found in the tropics. Look, for example, at the bright colors of the New Guinea birdwing, above left. Plant growth is very thick in the tropics. The animals and insects must be large and brightly colored so that they can find the members of their own species in order to mate.

The brimstone butterfly, pictured on the lower left, is found throughout Europe and northern Africa. Notice how closely its wings resemble leaves. The brimstone's coloring gives it protection from predators when this butterfly hibernates among ivy leaves.

We have seen the development of a butterfly, starting from an egg, moving on to an ever-hungry caterpillar, stopping as a motionless pupa, and finally emerging as a beautiful butterfly. Its rapid growth, variety of forms, and startling colors make the butterfly in all its stages one of the most interesting insects to watch.

45

GLOSSARY

antennae: moveable sensory organs that extend from the heads of insects and other animals

brush feet: the extremely short front legs of butterflies in the family *Nymphalidae*

camouflage: blending in with one's surroundings

chrysalis: a hard, protective shell that forms over the pupa

claspers: small, clawlike structures used in mating that extend from the end of a male butterfly's body

compound eye: an eye that is made up of many small lenses

family: a scientific grouping of related animals or plants

fertilize: to unite male and female reproductive cells so that an embryo may develop

gland: a cell or group of cells inside an animal's body that gives out chemical substances it creates

hibernate: to pass the winter in an inactive state. During hibernation all body functions slow down.

larva: a stage of metamorphosis when the insect is wormlike and has no wings

membrane: a thin layer of material, usually of animal or plant origin

metamorphosis: the series of changes that take place in some insects' development from egg to larva to pupa to adult

migratory: an animal that moves to a new living area, usually seasonally

molting: when an animal regularly sheds an outer layer of skin, feathers, or hair

nectar: a sweet liquid found in plants

ocelli: simple eyes that can only distinguish light from dark

pigment: color-creating chemicals in animals and plants

pollen: fine yellow "dust" on a seed plant, containing male reproductive cells

pollination: the transfer of pollen, containing male reproductive cells, to the female parts of a flower

predator: an animal that kills other animals for food

proboscis: any long, flexible snout on an animal. The proboscis of a butterly is a tube that is used to suck nectar.

prolegs: fleshy legs found on some insect larvae

pupa: the stage between the larva and the adult in the metamorphosis of some insects

segment: one of the 13 equal sections making up the body of a caterpillar

species: a group of animals or plants that share similar characteristics

sperm: male reproductive cells

veins: hardened tubes that stiffen the wings of an insect

INDEX

ABOUT THE AUTHORS

Heiderose and Andreas Fischer-Nagel received degrees in biology from the University of Berlin. Their special interests include animal behavior, wildlife protection, and environmental control. The Fischer-Nagels have collaborated as authors and photographers on several internationally successful science books for children. They attribute the success of their books to their "love of children and of our threatened environment" and believe that "children learning to respect nature today are tomorrow's protectors of nature."

The Fischer-Nagels live in Germany with their daughters, Tamarica and Cosmea Désirée.